SandCastle 3

How Do You Feel?

I Feel Safe

Kelly Doudna

Published by SandCastle™, an imprint of ABDO Publishing Company, 4940 Viking Drive, Edina, Minnesota 55435.

Printed in the United States.

Photo credits: Adobe Image Library, Corel, Digital Stock, Digital Vision, PhotoDisc

Library of Congress Cataloging-in-Publication Data

Doudna, Kelly, 1963-
    I feel safe / Kelly Doudna.
      p. cm. -- (How do you feel?)
    Summary: In photographs and simple text, children tell what makes
them feel safe, such as crossing the street with the crossing guard.
    ISBN 1-57765-191-X
    1. Security (Psychology) in children--Juvenile literature.
[1. Security (Psychology) 2. Safety.] I. Title. II. Series:
Doudna, Kelly, 1963- How do you feel?
BF723.S22D68 1998
152.4--dc21
                                      98-26689
                                         CIP
                                         AC

The SandCastle concept, content, and reading method have been reviewed and approved by a national advisory board including literacy specialists, librarians, elementary school teachers, early childhood education professionals, and parents.

Let Us Know

After reading the book, SandCastle would like you to tell us your stories about reading. What is your favorite page? Was there something hard that you needed help with? Share the ups and downs of learning to read. We want to hear from you! To get posted on the Abdo Publishing Company Web site, send us email at:

sandcastle@abdopub.com

About SandCastle™
Nonfiction books for the beginning reader

- Basic concepts of phonics are incorporated with integrated language methods of reading instruction. Most words are short, and phrases, letter sounds, and word sounds are repeated.

- Readability is determined by the number of words in each sentence, the number of characters in each word, and word lists based on curriculum frameworks.

- Full-color photography reinforces word meanings and concepts.

- "Words I Can Read" list at the end of each book teaches basic elements of grammar, helps the reader recognize the words in the text, and builds vocabulary.

- Reading levels are indicated by the number of flags on the castle.

Look for more SandCastle books in these three reading levels:

Level 1 (one flag)	**Level 2** (two flags)	**Level 3** (three flags)
SandCastle 1	SandCastle 2	SandCastle 3
Grades Pre-K to K 5 or fewer words per page	**Grades K to 1** 5 to 10 words per page	**Grades 1 to 2** 10 to 15 words per page

I feel safe when I walk with Grandpa.

I know I should not walk alone.

I feel safe when the crossing guard helps me cross the street.

I feel safe when I wear my helmet and Dad helps me ride my bike.

I feel safe when I swim with my parents.

They will take care of me.

I feel safe when I swing next to my older brother.

I feel safe when I ride the big Ferris wheel with Mom and Dad.

I feel safe when I hold on
tight to the merry-go-round.

I feel safe when I am tucked in my bed.

I feel safe with my family.

I know they will protect me.

Words I Can Read

Nouns
A noun is a person, place, or thing

bed (BED) p. 19
bike (BIKE) p. 9
brother (BRUHTH-ur) p. 13
care (KAIR) p. 11
crossing guard
  (KRAWSS-ing gard) p. 7
Dad (DAD) pp. 9, 15
family (FAM-uh-lee) p. 21

Ferris wheel
  (FER-iss weel) p. 15
Grandpa
  (GRAND-pah) p. 5
helmet (HEL-mit) p. 9
merry-go-round
  (MER-ee-goh-round) p. 17
Mom (MOM) p. 15
street (STREET) p. 7

Plural Nouns
A plural noun is more than one
person, place, or thing

parents (PAIR-uhntss) p. 11

Pronouns
A pronoun is a word that replaces a noun

I (EYE) pp. 5, 7, 9, 11, 13, 15,
  17, 19, 21

me (MEE) pp. 7, 9, 11, 21
they (THAY) pp. 11, 21

22

Verbs

A verb is an action or being word

am (AM) p. 19
cross (KRAWSS) p. 7
feel (FEEL) pp. 5, 7, 9, 11,
   13, 15, 17, 19, 21
helps (HELPSS) pp. 7, 9
hold (HOHLD) p. 17
know (NOH) pp. 5, 21
protect (pruh-TEKT) p. 21
ride (RIDE) pp. 9, 15

should (SHUD) p. 5
swim (SWIM) p. 11
swing (SWING) p. 13
take (TAYK) p. 11
tucked (TUHKT) p. 19
walk (WAWK) p. 5
wear (WAIR) p. 9
will (WIL) pp. 11, 21

Adjectives

An adjective describes something

alone (uh-LONE) p. 5
big (BIG) p. 15
my (MYE) pp. 9, 11, 13, 19, 21

older (OHLD-ur) p. 13
safe (SAYF) pp. 5, 7, 9, 11,
   13, 15, 17, 19, 21

Adverbs

An adverb tells how, when, or where
something happens

tight (TITE) p. 17

23

Glossary

crossing guard - Someone who helps people cross the street.

Ferris wheel - A large, upright wheel with seats hung on it, used as a fun ride.

helmet - A hard hat that protects your head.

merry-go-round - A round platform that spins.